D1716358

CONTEMPORARY MUSICIANS
AND THEIR MUSIC™

Usher

Dave Rodney

The Rosen Publishing Group, Inc., New York

Special thanks to Elaine Perkins, who inspired me to write; to Sylvia Rhone, Merlin Bobb, and Timmy Regisford, who created my first music opportunity; and to a supportive team—Victoria Harper, Abigail Adams, Anthony Turner, Keith "Doc" Clarke, Clyde Cadogan, and Carol Kirk—thanks so much for being there, no matter the weather

Published in 2007 by The Rosen Publishing Group, Inc.
29 East 21st Street, New York, NY 10010

First Edition

Library of Congress Cataloging-in-Publication Data

Rodney, Dave.
Usher/Dave Rodney.—1st ed.
    p. cm.—(Contemporary musicians and their music)
Includes discography (p.   ), bibliographical references (p.   ), and index.
ISBN 1-4042-0711-2 (library binding)
1. Usher. 2. Singers—United States—Biography. 3. Rhythm and blues musicians—United States—Biography. I. Title. II. Series.
ML420.U77R63 2007
782.421643092—dc22

                                                      2006003825

Manufactured in Malaysia

On the cover: Usher performs at the 2005 World Music Awards at the Kodak Theatre in Hollywood, California, on August 31, 2005.

Contents

Introduction

The 2004 American Music Awards show was a coronation for Usher. The then twenty-six-year-old contemporary R & B singer walked away with four major awards, which were determined by a poll of 20,000 music buyers. His awards included Favorite Male Artist in both the pop/rock and soul/R & B categories. Within the next few months, he won many other music awards, for a total of eighty-seven, confirming his status at the pinnacle of the popular music industry.

Usher's infectious grooves and electrifying stage performances have made him one of the most successful recording artists ever.

The numerous awards provide only a limited measure of Usher's global superstardom. From chart-topping hits that dominate radio playlists to sold-out concerts and young ladies swooning at his electrifying presence, the young singer is enjoying the kind of success that most recording artists can only dream of. This popularity, in addition to his dazzling dancing skills, mix of romantic and party tunes, and seemingly endless store of energy and confidence, has drawn comparisons to Michael Jackson, one of his childhood musical idols. Various music commentators consider him the new king of pop.

Like the careers of others who have achieved his level of fame, Usher's rise to superstardom is a combination of talent, luck, hard work, and sacrifice. In his ten-plus years in the business, he has seen his share of ups and downs. Through it all, he has pushed toward his goal with confidence and determination.

Usher began his career as an ambitious teen in search of an image. Today, he is the reigning king of R & B, who proclaims himself "Mr. Entertainment" and "the ultimate entertainer." Having sold millions of albums worldwide and won every major music award, he now sets his sights on becoming a giant in film, fashion, and the business world.

Chapter One

Great Expectations

Usher was born Usher Raymond IV on October 14, 1978, in Dallas, Texas, to Usher Raymond III and Jonnetta Patton. Within a year of his birth, his parents divorced and his mother moved with Usher to Chattanooga, Tennessee. There, he was surrounded by an extended family that included grandparents, aunts, uncles, and cousins, all of whom lavished him with attention. According to his mom, Usher was a fun-loving and mischievous kid who was always getting into trouble.

Usher's interest in show business began at an early age. Singing became his constant hobby, as other pastimes, such as basketball or football, never kept his focus for long. He claimed the spotlight at family gatherings, which often centered around

Usher sings with his childhood idol Michael Jackson at New York City's Madison Square Garden on September 7, 2001, at a concert marking Jackson's thirtieth anniversary as a solo performer.

music and dance. Usher credits the 1970 Jackson 5 hit single "I Want You Back" as the song that spurred his interest in singing. As he told *Entertainment Weekly* in 1998, "That was my beginning, even before I started singing in church. I used to hum and sing with the radio, but I wasn't really serious about it. But when I heard that song, I was inspired." In addition to Michael Jackson, he enjoyed listening to Prince; Marvin Gaye; Stevie Wonder; Bobby Brown; Luther Vandross; Parliament; and Earth, Wind & Fire.

But it was in church that Usher honed his natural talent. He began singing with the St. Elmo's Missionary Baptist Church youth choir when he was six years old. His mother, who was the choir director, recalls that even then Usher was very passionate about practicing and performing.

The Grooming of a Star

Jonnetta Patton recognized early that her son had an exceptional talent to match his great passion. Therefore, she committed herself to giving him greater exposure than he could get in her church choir. Accordingly, she began entering him in talent competitions by the time he was nine years old. This turned out to be a smart move. Usher enjoyed tremendous success in the competitions, which boosted his confidence.

At the age of twelve, Usher earned a spot in a local R & B group called Nu Beginnings, which recorded an album that was distributed locally. However, his mother pulled him from the group because she didn't think that it was the best showcase for her son. She was convinced he had the makings of a star solo artist. Usher was crushed by his mother's decision. "He told me that I had destroyed his whole life," Patton told MTV in 2005. Shortly thereafter, she moved the family, which by then included

Usher's mother made many sacrifices to give her son the chance to realize his dream. She continues to play a prominent role in his career, and he often refers to her as his best friend.

a younger brother, James Lackey, to Atlanta, Georgia. At the time, Atlanta was quickly developing a reputation as the new hub of African American pop music.

In Atlanta, where he attended North Springs High School, Usher continued to enter and excel in talent shows. Soon, there was quite a buzz about the lanky teenager, especially after he began winning round after round on *Star Search*, a nationally televised competition. (He eventually became the male teen vocalist champion.) It was during a *Star Search* appearance that he was spotted by Bryant Reid, brother of LaFace Records copresident Antonio "L. A." Reid. Usher was only thirteen years old at the time. Impressed, Bryant Reid arranged an audition for Usher with his brother and Kenneth

"Babyface" Edmonds, the other copresident, at the record company's Atlanta headquarters. There, Usher sang Tevin Campbell's "Tomorrow," which was one of his favorite songs at the time. "I thought he was amazing," L. A. Reid told CNN's Paula Zahn in April 2005. "I brought in several people from the office and he sang for them and mesmerized all the girls, and that day, I offered him a recording contract."

Although they were impressed by Usher's vocal talent, the LaFace executives didn't think that his choirboy image would play well in a market that was dominated by the in-your-face brashness of hip-hop. So they set out to toughen his image by sending the fourteen-year-old to "flavor camp"—essentially to live with Sean "Diddy" Combs, then the hottest new producer, in New York City. The plan was to groom Usher into an artist with a more distinctive edge. As Patton told Zahn, "They wanted Usher to be this bad boy."

The First Attempt

Usher was almost fifteen years old when his debut single made the R & B charts in late 1993. It was "Call Me a Mack," from the movie soundtrack of *Poetic Justice*. With this song, Usher boastfully introduced himself to the world as a smooth-talking ladies' man. The following year, his self-titled debut album, executive produced by Diddy, then known as Puff Daddy, was released. It was filled with sexually suggestive love songs that extended the fabricated bad boy/lover man image. The album rose to number 25 on the Billboard Top R & B/Hip-Hop Album chart and number 167 on the Billboard 200 pop albums chart, on the strength of three singles: "Can U Get Wit It," "The Many Ways," and "Think of You," a top 10 R & B hit featuring a rap by Biz Markie.

These results would have been considered promising for most new artists. However, in Usher's case, the expectations for the album were very high, and so the results proved disappointing. Clearly, the attempt at rebranding Usher failed—perhaps even backfired. Music critics, as well as the general public, weren't convinced by the bad boy/ladies' man postures of the baby-faced teen. It didn't help that soon after the album was released, puberty robbed Usher of his clear, distinct, high-pitched tones. As he struggled to deal with his voice change, many people in the music industry began wondering whether he had been a bad investment.

Although he, too, was disappointed by the number of sales, Usher treated the lackluster performance of his first album as a learning experience. He continued to build his musical profile by recording jingles for Coca-Cola and working with other artists to

Sean Combs (*right*) was the first producer with whom Usher worked as a solo artist. Prior to producing Usher, Combs had enjoyed tremendous success launching the careers of a number of R & B and hip-hop stars, including Mary J. Blige, Jodeci, and the Notorious B.I.G.

perfect his range. He joined up with several established and up-and-coming R & B artists under the name Black Men United to record a song called "U Will Know" for the *Jason's Lyric* sound-track. This song enjoyed moderate success, reaching number 28 on the Billboard Hot 100 chart in late 1994 and number 5 on the Hot R & B/Hip-Hop Songs chart. Over the next three years, Usher honed his skills as a stage performer. He concentrated on his schoolwork while making preparations for his second album.

Chapter Two

The Second Time Around

Despite their disappointment with the weak sales of Usher's debut album, the executives at LaFace Records remained confident of the singer's star potential. Consequently, they charted a new path for Usher, hiring voice coaches to help him harness his newer, deeper voice. They also gave him greater creative control over his music and hired superproducer Jermaine Dupri to help guide his career.

At sixteen, Usher went to live and work with Dupri for about six months. The two spent a lot of time club-hopping, shopping, researching, and developing new images to reframe his career. "I noticed that he had the hunger and the want to be a star," Dupri told CNN's Paula Zahn in 2005. "He was looking for a lot

Jermaine Dupri *(left)* and Usher quickly developed a good working relationship. Before working with Usher, Dupri had produced hits for Kris Kross, Xscape, Da Brat, and TLC. He remains one of the most successful and sought-after record producers.

of direction and somebody to help him get to places that he wanted to go." Dupri turned out to be the right person for the job.

My Way

The first fruit of Usher's partnership with Jermaine Dupri was a resounding success. In 1997, Usher released the single "You Make Me Wanna," which he cowrote with Dupri. The song rocketed up the Billboard Hot R & B/Hip-Hop Songs chart, peaking at the number 1 position, where it remained for eleven consecutive weeks. It reached number 2 on the Hot 100 chart. In the wake of the popularity of the single, the release of Usher's second album was a highly anticipated event for a growing fan base.

The album *My Way* was released later that year, just after Usher had graduated from high school. It benefited from the contributions of several of the recording industry's most successful producers, including L. A. Reid and Babyface. One of the hottest albums of 1997, it blends silky vocals and seductive lyrics over compelling grooves, accented by elements of hip-hop. Usher cowrote six of the album's nine tracks with Dupri. Like "You Make Me Wanna," most of the tracks were mid-tempo ballads. The notable exception was the experimental hip-hop-styled "Nice 'N' Slow," which topped the Hot 100 chart in March 1998. The title track climbed to number 2 in August 1998. The album also included a remake of Midnight Star's R & B classic "Slow Jam," featuring fellow teenage star Monica. *My Way* eventually sold more than three million copies, and it made quite a splash in the United Kingdom and Canada, as well.

Usher received his first Grammy nomination as Best Male R & B Vocal Performance for "You Make Me Wanna," which later won the Soul Train Music Award for Best Male R & B/Soul Single.

Usher poses with Cher at the Billboard Awards in Las Vegas, Nevada, on December 7, 1998, after being named Artist of the Year.

Finally, Usher had delivered the successful album to match the great expectations that came with his label deal. Music critics attributed the success of *My Way* to its being more age-appropriate than the first album, *Usher*, and having a more youthful tease and curiosity. He was now on center stage, commanding a lot of attention. His boyish smile, vigorous enthusiasm, and slick music videos won new waves of fans. Usher had indeed arrived. He had become a new master of contemporary R & B, and he had his sights set on a whole lot more. "I guess I am an usher in a way," he told *Jet* magazine. "I'm ushering in something very new, very fresh. Hopefully, it'll have longevity. That's my goal. I don't want to be stereotyped as just a hip-hop artist or an R & B artist. I want to cover it all."

With his first album, Usher's performance circuit was limited primarily to school tours and back-to-school jams. As his stature rapidly grew, he graduated to headlining his own concerts at mid-sized theaters. He began traveling with an entourage and required several security guards to prevent him from being mobbed by excited fans. His fame bloomed further. In his live performances, his playful tease seemed to always tantalize a crowd.

At a 1998 concert at the legendary Apollo Theatre in Harlem, New York, Usher wowed a packed audience with a dazzling performance. Many people in the music industry mark that event as the moment Usher proved he was a well-rounded entertainer and not just a studio singer. Speaking about the performance, Usher later told MTV, "When you come to Apollo, you gotta sing, you gotta dance, you gotta give it up to the audience. They want to see that, and to get the response I got, when the song came on I came sliding out, all the audience bumrushed the stage. It's like, '. . . I think I'm a superstar.'"

Usher's star turn at the Apollo landed him opening spots on tours by Sean Combs, Mary J. Blige, and Janet Jackson, exposing him to larger live audiences. With these appearances, Usher established himself as a chest-baring, ab-flexing showman, much to the delight of his growing number of fans. He was not

WHAT IS R & B?

The great jazz singer Louis Armstrong once said that if you have to ask what jazz is, you'll never know. The same can be said of R & B, which is so varied that it isn't easily described. Today, "R & B" is a catchall phrase for African American pop music. As such, it includes Motown classics of the 1960s, such as recordings by the Jackson 5, Diana Ross and the Supremes, and Marvin Gaye; seventies funk, as recorded by Parliament-Funkadelic; the soul stylings of Aretha Franklin, James Brown, Luther Vandross, and Peabo Bryson; jazzy soul, which includes music by Anita Baker and Will Downing; the new jack swing of Bobby Brown and Teddy Riley's Guy; and hip-hop/soul, such as recordings by Usher and Mary J. Blige.

At it's broadest, R & B can be said to include hip-hop, although the latter has, since its origin in the late 1970s, developed an identity all its own. Nevertheless, the line between the two forms is blurry at best: Hip-hop music is often anchored on samples of classic R & B grooves and hooks, and contemporary R & B is heavily accented by elements of hip-hop and is more likely than not to include a rap break.

"R & B" is short for "rhythm and blues," a term coined in the late 1940s to describe the popular black music of the time, which was a fusion of swing jazz rhythms and the lyrical and vocal patterns of the blues. Today, many people use the long form (rhythm and blues) to describe the original sound, thereby distinguishing it from contemporary R & B. However, this distinction is not universally accepted.

continued on following page

continued from previous page

Whatever the form, however, most R & B tunes are rhythm-driven, feature demonstrably emotive vocalizing (often with a call-and-response interplay between lead singer and backing vocals), and share a common instrumentation that usually includes a drum set, bass and rhythm guitars, keyboards, and horns, most often saxophones.

shy to show off his body—sculpted by a demanding workout schedule—which quickly gained him the status of a sex symbol.

Through it all, Usher's mother, who is also his manager, maintained a strong presence in his life. She encouraged him to remain humble and to respect his audience, his peers, and his work. Patton kept him focused spiritually and helped him manage his money. She wanted to ensure that he did not make the same mistakes of other R & B and hip-hop stars who had suffered humbling financial crises, including bankruptcy, after their rise to fame.

Usher's Diversity and Depth

The success of *My Way* created new opportunities for Usher. In late 1997, he made his acting debut on the television sitcom *Moesha*, starring fellow teenage R & B sensation Brandy Norwood. Abounding with confidence, Usher told *Jet* magazine,

"I'm a natural. I have a talent to take words off paper and relate to it," despite not having had formal training as an actor.

Other TV roles followed, including a recurring role in the daytime drama *The Bold and the Beautiful*, an appearance in the family series *Promised Land*, and a part in the Disney movie *Geppetto*. In 1998, Usher made his big-screen debut in *The Faculty*, in which he plays a football star at a high school that is controlled by aliens. The following year, he appeared in two more films, *Light It Up*, his first starring role, and *She's All That*.

The demands of his burgeoning acting career meant that Usher had little time to work on new songs. However, the singer-turned-actor knew that he had to maintain a presence on the music scene, so he released *Live* in 1999. The album is a collection of concert recordings culled from his tours, as well as remixes of hit singles "My Way," "Nice & Slow," and "You Make Me Wanna." Among the surprises were a medley of hit songs previously recorded by Bobby Brown and collaborations with a number of guest vocalists, including Jagged Edge, Trey Lorenz, Shanice, Twista, Manuel Seal, and Lil' Kim.

Despite the additional star power, *Live* failed to achieve the success of *My Way*. It reached only number 73 on the Billboard 200 and number 30 on the Top R & B/Hip-Hop Albums chart.

Usher *(third from left)* poses with fellow cast members of the sci-fi/horror film *The Faculty* during a promotional event at Planet Hollywood in New York City on November 13, 1998. The other cast members are *(from left to right)* Jordana Brewster, Shawn Hatosy, Clea DuVall, Josh Hartnett, and Elijah Woods.

However, neither Usher nor his record company was discouraged by the weak sales because the live album was intended to be a filler project until Usher had time to record his true follow-up album. It was, nevertheless, an important album for Usher's fans, as it documented how much the singer had reworked the songs and signaled his musical evolution.

Meanwhile, Usher began to get involved with various civic projects. Embracing his status as a role model, he became a national spokesperson for the U.S. Department of Transportation's Get Big On Safety campaign. He also participated in the National Basketball Association's (NBA) Stay In School program by performing at several of the teams' jamborees, entertaining students while reminding them of the importance of education.

8701

In 2000, Usher finally returned to the studio to record the much-awaited follow-up album, scheduled for release in early 2001. However, many of the songs from the album, which was called *All About U*, were leaked on Napster, a Web site that allows users to share digital copies of recorded music. Furious, Usher pulled the plug on the project and recorded a new album.

That album was called *8701*. It was a smash hit, climbing to number 4 on the Billboard 200 album chart and number 3 on the Top R & B/Hip-Hop Albums chart. It also broadened Usher's international appeal. It topped the charts in both Canada and the United Kingdom and sold very well in Australia. The album *8701* spawned four major hits: "Pop Ya Collar," "U Turn," "U Remind Me," and "U Don't Have to Call," the last two of which earned Usher the Grammy Award for Best Male R & B Vocal in 2002 and 2003 respectively. Usher joined Luther Vandross and

Stevie Wonder as the only artists to have won that award in consecutive years.

Things were going great for Usher. His album *8701* and the supporting tour confirmed his superstardom, and the offers for film roles continued to pour in. (He appeared in the western *Texas Rangers* in 2001.) He was also enjoying the spoils of his success. In 2003, he bought a mansion for $2.8 million in Atlanta, Georgia, and several cars. He quickly earned a reputation for his love of shopping, especially for chic European designer clothes. "I'm a flamboyant type of guy, a cooler version of Liberace," Usher told *Interview*. As one-half of one of the most high-profile R & B couples, he also appeared to be lucky in love. He was dating Rozonda "Chilli" Thomas of TLC, whom he has called the love of his life. That relationship would serve as a major influence in Usher's future career.

Usher's stage sets and costumes have become more elaborate as his stature has grown. He changes costumes frequently during his concerts, alternating between hip-hop gear and slick designer clothes. He sometimes rips off his T-shirt to expose his well-defined abs.

Chapter Three

The Year That Belonged to Usher

The crazy thing about success in the music business is that once an artist crosses a certain threshold, future projects that fall short of that mark—no matter how spectacular—are often considered failures. In addition to the fame and fortune gained from a successful record, the artist usually earns a greater degree of creative control, which increases the pressure to meet or beat his or her previous sales mark.

For Usher, who began working on his next album in 2003, the pressure was intensified by the general feeling among his record executives and musical collaborators that, despite his success, he needed to show an edge. Mimi Valdez, editor of *Vibe* magazine, summed up that view in a conversation with CNN's Paula Zahn:

Usher and his girlfriend, Chilli, arrive at the screening of his DVD *Usher Live: Evolution 8701* at the State Theater in New York City on November 11, 2002.

Usher "didn't really have a story. There wasn't really anything interesting about him." Although Usher had full creative control, his label chief gave him one clear directive: Usher should use the new album to let the public know exactly who he was.

Confessions

Unlike the preparations for his debut album, Usher didn't have to fabricate that edge. He was now twenty-five years old and had experienced of lot of things since those early days. His life and, in particular, his relationship with Chilli had given him all the edge he would need. The two broke up in January 2004, after months of discussions and quarrels about the state of their relationship—Usher admitted that he had not always been faithful. The breakup provided much fodder for the drama-hungry entertainment press. More important, it was the primary inspiration for Usher's career album, *Confessions*, which was released on March 23, 2004.

In *Confessions*, Usher reveals himself as a player—a guy who has several girlfriends at the same time. The player is a recurring image in hip-hop and modern R & B and is often regarded with awe whether he is being praised or criticized. What separates Usher's treatment of the subject from those of many other artists is that *his* player is vulnerable; he is subject to being hurt by his own cheating as well as by his unfaithful partner. In essence, as the lyrics to songs such as "Burn," "Caught Up," "Truth Hurt," and the title track show, Usher's edge was that he was a player with a sensitive side.

Dominating the Charts and the Award Ceremonies

Confessions sold a whopping 1.1 million copies in its first week, topping both the pop and R & B charts. Released a week earlier, the album's lead single, "Yeah," featuring Lil' Jon and Ludacris, quickly shot up to the top of the Billboard Hot 100 chart, where it stayed for twelve weeks. In May, he had three songs in the top 10, a feat last accomplished by the Bee Gees in the 1970s. By the

Usher poses backstage with several of the eleven awards that he won at the Billboard Music Awards at the MGM Grand Garden Arena in Las Vegas, Nevada, on December 8, 2004.

end of the year, *Confessions* had yielded four number 1 singles— "Yeah"; "Burn"; "Confessions Part II"; and "My Boo," a duet with Alicia Keys—a first for any artist in thirty-four years. Combined, these singles kept Usher on top of the charts for twenty-eight weeks in 2004, making him the only artist in history to hold the number 1 position for more than half a year. *Confessions* and its singles also ruled pop music charts in many other countries, including Australia, Norway, Switzerland, Canada, and the United Kingdom. As of this writing, the album has sold more than fifteen million copies.

On June 29, Usher won two awards (Best Male R & B Artist and Viewers Choice) at the BET Music Awards in Hollywood, California. Those wins launched an incredible awards season for

Usher—lasting well into 2005—during which the singer walked away with many of the most-coveted awards in the United States. He also picked up music awards in many other countries. In addition to eleven Billboard Music Awards, three Grammy Awards, and four American Music Awards, Usher received four World Music Awards and was named Top Male Artist at the first annual Nordic Music Awards, which are based on the votes of fans in Norway, Denmark, and Sweden. After performing with Usher at the 2005 Grammy Awards, James Brown, who is known as the godfather of soul, proclaimed Usher to be the godson of soul.

On the Road

On August 5, 2004, Usher kicked off the Truth Tour, which took him to sixty-four cities, including stops throughout Europe, Africa, Asia, and Australia. All across the globe, the concerts sold out so quickly that Usher and Kanye West, his opening act, had to add dates in several cities. According to *Forbes* magazine, the tour grossed more than $20 million.

Now a full-fledged headliner, Usher spared no expense to dazzle his audiences with elaborate stage sets, spectacular pyrotechnics, mammoth video screens, eight dancers, flashy costumes, and his band, Four Pieces and a Biscuit. Writing

Usher performs a backflip on stage during his Truth Tour concert at the Mariner Arena in Baltimore, Maryland, on August 6, 2004. He is an energetic showman who packs a lot of action and fan interaction into his live performances.

about a concert at the Phillips Arena in Atlanta, Georgia, Rosemary Jean-Louis said that there were plenty of "hot and bothered, frenzied teenage" girls. She also noted that the "mothers and fathers of teenage girls, single thirtysomething men and couples appear to be admirers, too. They cram the seats at the virtually sold-out Atlanta show." Of Usher's performance she wrote, "But it is Usher who captivates, pouring through his greatest hits with the stamina of an Energizer Bunny. Even during a music break for his song 'You Remind Me' he is doing handstands and popping and locking." (In October 2005, Usher released a three-disc DVD set called *Behind the Truth*, which includes a recording of that concert and behind-the-scene peeks at his life on the road.)

Confessions and the Truth Tour made Usher the top-selling and most visible solo performer in the music business in 2004. His song "Yeah" was by far the most played song of the year and one of the most popular cell phone ring tones. At the end of the year, entertainment commentators were proclaiming him the new king of pop, a rewarding accolade for someone who was daring enough to bill himself as the ultimate entertainer. Successful and becoming rich very fast, Usher had dreams of even greater glory.

Chapter Four

Branching Out

On March 5, 2005, Usher told fans at a concert in Puerto Rico that this appearance would be his last live performance for the year. He was going to take a long-needed vacation, during which he would travel all over the world. Of his future career plans he said: "I'm a businessman before I'm a musician. I'll be doing movies. I got a record label, Us Records. I want you to trust me when I tell you I've got some amazing artists on my label. This is not a goodbye. This is not a farewell. This is a 'I'll see you later!'"

Investments and Movies

Usher is serious about being a businessman, and he is not embarrassed about discussing himself as a brand. His current

Usher laughs at a news conference introducing the new owners of the Cleveland Cavaliers on March 1, 2005. Since becoming a co-owner of the NBA franchise, Usher has played an active role in building fan support for the team.

role models include Oprah Winfrey, Sean Combs, Martha Stewart, and Russell Simmons, all of whom have used their fame to launch into a wide assortment of business ventures. Around the time he was launching the Truth Tour, Mastercard unveiled a prepaid debit card bearing a photograph of the R & B superstar.

But Usher's business ventures go far beyond such endorsement deals. He owns an office complex in Atlanta with his mother. His record company and her management company are situated there. In February 2005, he invested about $9 million to become a part owner of the Cleveland Cavaliers, a pro basketball team. According to *Forbes* magazine, he invested another $1 million as seed capital to open a new bank. As of this writing, he has plans to launch a line of formal menswear. He is also financing various film projects.

The first of those movies is *In the Mix*, which was released in November 2005. In a role that was created specifically for him, Usher makes his first appearance as a leading man. He plays Darrell, a DJ whom a mob boss hires to be his daughter's bodyguard. Other movies in the works include *The Ballad of Walter Holmes*, a portrayal of the life of an R & B singer; an adaptation of the Broadway musical *Dreamgirls*, which will also star Beyoncé; and an update of Elvis Presley's *Jailhouse Rock*.

Giving Back

In addition to his business ventures, Usher has stepped up his involvement in charities. On June 10, 2005, he launched the New Look Foundation as his endeavor to use "education and real world experiences as vehicles to expose young people to valuable life skills, career development and social responsibility opportunities," as stated on the foundation's Web site. The following month, the foundation held its first Camp New Look at Morehouse College in Atlanta. During the two-week camp, 150 young people aspiring for careers in show business and sports attended work sessions and classes that taught them effective ways to pursue their dreams. They also learned about the

FILM CREDITS

Moesha (TV series, 1997–1998)
The Bold and the Beautiful (TV series, 1998)
The Faculty (movie, 1998)
The Promised Land (TV series, 1999)
She's All That (movie, 1999)
Light It Up (movie, 1999)
Sabrina the Teenage Witch (TV series, 2002)
Geppetto (TV movie, 2000)
Texas Rangers (movie, 2001)
The Twilight Zone (TV series, 2002)
7th Heaven (TV series, 2002)
Soul Food (TV series, 2003)
In the Mix (movie, 2005)

vast array of behind-the-scenes career opportunities in the entertainment business. At the end of the two weeks, the campers used the skills they learned to produce and stage an elaborate halftime show for a celebrity basketball game that was held as a fund-raiser for the foundation. To the surprise of the campers and many observers, Usher took a very hands-on role in the camp.

Following 2005's Hurricane Katrina, Usher took a break from his vacation from the stage to headline a fund-raising concert for the hurricane victims. Through his foundation, he also teamed up with Freddie Mac and Hibernia Bank to launch Project Restart, which aims to find new homes for 1,000 of the displaced families.

Usher is proud of his charity work and embraces his stature as a role model. He refers to his foundation as his most challenging work to date. That's a modest claim for the new king of pop.

Offstage

Some music lovers may ask what factors contributed to Usher's phenomenal success. Was it sheer luck, or was it a strategic plan? The realistic answer is that his successes are as much due to his raw, natural ability as they are the product of his determination and drive and his mother's steadfast support. Another important consideration was Usher's ability to attract the attention

Usher *(center)* poses with some of the kids from Camp New Look at Morehouse College in Atlanta, Georgia, on July 23, 2004, following the New Look first annual celebrity basketball game.

of some of the hottest producers and record label executives. One part of the equation hardly works without the others, but when all the elements come together, explosive success such as Usher's is the outcome.

Another frequently asked question is whether success has changed Usher. Yes, it probably has changed him a bit, as it does many other artists who have achieved the elusive status of superstardom. Being a superstar today also means being a target for all kinds of strangers who come with various agendas, not all of them benevolent. In response, many artists build an almost impenetrable shield around them to protect themselves. Sometimes this protective shield leads to paranoia, and they feel people are out to get them.

Usher, by his own admission, can be difficult. As his mother explained to *Essence* magazine in June 2005, "When things go wrong, Usher comes down on everybody. Then I'll remind him of where he came from, that there was a time when he didn't have a record deal. I make sure he doesn't think he's so big he can talk to people any kind of way." However, Usher's detractors say that he has grown arrogant to the point where he is verbally abusive to people. This image is of course different from the one portrayed in music videos where Usher is seen as the dashing, dimpled pretty boy whom women adore. Despite his awesome achievements, Usher is quick to point out that he is only human and susceptible to imperfection and mistakes. For example, although he expresses great appreciation for his fans, he admits that he sometimes shows up very late for meet-and-greet sessions because he has been out shopping.

Since his breakup with Chilli, Usher has dated a number of women, including supermodel Naomi Campbell. However, he says he is not ready to settle down right now, despite his

Usher mixes it up with the audience at Andre Agassi's Tenth Grand Slam for Children show at the MGM Grand Garden Arena on October 1, 2005. With his engaging tunes and commanding stage presence, Usher has established himself as the latest in a long line of engaging male R&B superstars.

grandmother's constant questions about when he is going to give her a great-grandchild.

The Future

As of this writing, Usher is renegotiating his recording contract with his label, now Sony BMG. According to *Forbes* magazine, he is seeking a multirecord deal worth $50 million. Usher plans to return to the studio between late 2006 and early 2007 to record his next album.

It has been an incredible rise to superstardom for the Chattanooga kid with the silky voice, boyish smile, and energetic dance steps. Although Usher proclaims himself to be the ultimate entertainer, he doesn't envision himself on stage past his forties. In the meantime, he's making the most of his reign as pop music's brightest star.

Timeline

1978   Usher is born on October 14 in Dallas, Texas.

1990   Usher joins an R & B group called Nu Beginnings; his mother moves the family to Atlanta, Georgia.

1992   Usher wins Male Teen Star on *Star Search* and lands a recording contract with LaFace Records.

1993   Usher releases his first single, "Call Me a Mack."

1994   Usher's first album is released.

1997   Usher scores his first R & B number 1 single with "You Make Me Wanna"; releases his second album, *My Way*; and makes his acting debut on *Moesha*.

1998   Usher wins his first Grammy Award and makes his big-screen debut in *The Faculty*.

1999   Usher releases *Live*; he appears in the movies *She's All That* and *Light It Up*.

2000   Usher releases *8701*.

2003   Usher starts a record company.

2004   Usher releases *Confessions* and launches the Truth Tour.

2005   Usher buys a stake in the Cleveland Cavaliers. He launches the New Look Foundation and Project Restart, and stars in the film *In the Mix*.

Discography

Albums

Usher (1994)

My Way (1997)

Live (1999)

8701 (2001)

Confessions (2004)

DVDs

Rhythm City Volume One: Caught Up (2005)

Behind the Truth (2005)

Glossary

accolade An expression of praise.

benevolent Good.

entourage A person's attendants or associates.

hone To sharpen.

locking Urban dance style characterized by locking arm positions in time to a beat.

phenomenal Unusual, amazing, exceedingly great.

popping An urban dance style characterized by tensing and releasing muscles to make them appear to pop.

pyrotechnics Fireworks and other chemical effects used onstage to create explosions and other special effects.

seed capital Money provided in the developmental stage of a business project.

For More Information

Cleveland Cavaliers

One Center Court

Cleveland, OH 44115-4001

Web site: http://www.nba.com/cavaliers/

LaFace/Zomba Records

137-139 West 25 Street, 9th Floor

New York, NY 10001

(212) 727-0016

Web site: http://www.laface.com

Usher's New Look, Inc.

2775 Cruse Road, Suite 901

Lawrenceville, GA 30044

Web site: http://www.ushersnewlook.org/home.html

Web Sites

Due to the changing nature of Internet links, the Rosen Publishing Group, Inc., has developed an online list of Web sites related to the subject of this book. This site is updated regularly. Please use this link to access the list:

http://www.rosenlinks.com/cmtm/usher

For Further Reading

Nickson, Chris. *Usher: The Godson of Soul*. New York, NY: Simon Spotlight, 2005.

Talmadge, Morgan. *Usher* (Celebrity Bios). New York, NY: Children's Press, 2001.

Torres, John. *Usher*. Hockessin, DE: Mitchell Lane Publishers, 2005.

Bibliography

Amber, Jeannine. "Growing Pains." *Essence*, June 2005, Vol. 36, No. 2, pp. 124–129.

Bryan Broadcasting. "Usher." Retrieved September 2005 (http://www.knde.com/candy-artists.php?artist = 8).

CNN People in the News. "Profiles of Mariah Carey and Usher," hosted by Paula Zahn. Aired April 30, 2005. Retrieved November 2005 (http://transcripts.cnn.com/TRANSCRIPTS/0504/30/pitn.01.html).

Galeschools.com. "Usher." Retrieved September 2005 (http://www.galeschools.com/black_history/bio/usher.htm).

Mayfield, Geoff. "Over the Counter: Usher Rides Rising Tide." *Billboard*, April 10, 2004, Vol. 116, No. 15, pp. 49–52.

MTVNews.com. "Mother Knows Best: Jonetta Patton Shares Stories About Her Son." Retrieved December 2005 (http://mtv.com/bands/u/usher/news_feature_052404/index4.jhtml).

Pulley, Brett. "Diamonds, Cars, and Confessions." Forbes.com. May 2005. Retrieved December 2005 (http://www.forbes.com/business/global/2005/0509/018.html).

Usherworld.com. "About Usher: Biography." Retrieved September 2005 (http://www.usherworld.com/about-biography.php).

Index

About the Author

Dave Rodney is a music and media marketing consultant based in the New York area. He was born in Jamaica and generated the first dance hall signing to Atlantic Records in 1988 with reggae artist Lt. Stitchie. He has executive produced several albums and has toured the world, promoting music and producing and staging concerts. He has also coordinated many music events such as the Sinbad Soul Music Festival, MTV's *Spring Break*, Motown's Soul by the Sea, and Hot 97 Hot Nights in Jamaica (of which Usher was a part). Rodney is currently a consultant for *Vibe* magazine.

Photo Credits

Cover, pp. 1, 4–5, 8, 13, 15, 17, 22, 24, 27, 29, 31, 36, 38, 40 © Getty Images; pp. 10, 34 © Associated Press, AP.

Designer: Gene Mollica; **Editor:** Wayne Anderson
Photo Researcher: Gene Mollica